THE COMPLETE BEGINNER'S GUIDE TO

Calligraphy

THE COMPLETE BEGINNER'S GUIDE TO

Calligraphy

p

This is a Parragon Publishing Book

This edition published in 2006

Parragon Publishing

Queen Street House

4 Queen Street

Bath BA1 1HE, UK

This edition designed by Design Principals

Text by Mary Noble

Calligraphy by Mary Noble

ISBN: 1-40547-134-4

Printed in China

Contents

Introduction

So, you want to do calligraphy? Welcome to a most rewarding pastime that will always provide you with outlets for your passion, from writing titles, labels and envelopes, to preparing works of art to be framed and displayed on the wall. The digital age ought to have made calligraphy redundant, but instead it has freed us from the drudgery of everyday text-writing and left calligraphers to focus on special occasions where the hand-made is valued and cherished.

The basics

Start with a few basic tools, and build up as your interest develops. Most items are available at art materials suppliers, or large stationers. Most important are:

Plain paper pad of thin plain white "layout" paper, or photocopy paper.

Plastic ruler with clear markings.

Pencil for ruling lines H or 2H stays sharper for longer than the standard HB.

Sharpener because blunt pencils are not accurate.

Masking Tape can be used for taping down your ink bottle and holding the paper in place.

Pens

Fiber-tipped pens are a good starter tool, easy to use and especially good to use on envelopes—replace them when they get blunt and be aware that the inks can fade.

Fountain pens come in sets of sizes and are convenient to use, with cartridge inks that will not spill.

Dip pens are the choice of professionals as they can be used with all kinds of paints and inks, as washing out and changing nib sizes is straightforward. They usually have some form of reservoir attached to the nib to hold the ink or paint.

Inks

Cartridges for fountain pens come in black and bright colors, the inks will fade over time so ideal for temporary work.

Bottled inks for dip pens are variable; beware anything containing shellac or acrylic, as these are better for background washes than for writing. Choose non-waterproof ink,

Japanese Sumi ink is best if you can get it, or Chinese or Indian inks. Test on your paper, as some inks "bleed" on some papers.

Paints

Watercolor paints are bright, transparent colors, easy to mix for calligraphy and come in tubes and pans; use them on white paper.

Designers' Gouaches are opaque colors that will show up on colored papers and backgrounds, and come in tubes for mixing with water to ink consistency.

Drawing board

Writing on a sloped surface allows better control of ink flow and better posture for the writer. Find a piece of plywood about A3 size and make a soft writing surface by padding it with 6 pages of newspaper, a top cover of white, and fix with masking tape. Prop the board up on books, on a table with good light.

Guard sheet

Keep a piece of paper under your writing hand at all times, to protect the writing page from both spatters and the oils from your hand, which will make the page slippery for the writing.

Glossary of terms

Arches: critical feature of construction in letters n and m in Foundational and Italic, which are very different.

Ascenders and descenders: the extensions as in b, h, g and y that go beyond the main body of the letters.

Counters: the inside parts of letters.

Majuscule: capital letters.

Margins: the free space which must surround a piece of writing on a page to allow the design to stand out.

Minuscule: small letters (lower case in typographic terms).

Nib-widths: the method we use to gain the right thickness for our letters, eg Uncial is 4 times the width of whatever pen you use, so 4 nib-widths.

Pen angle: where the nib's edge sits on the page relative to the writing line. In this book we measure 15, 30 and 45 degrees up from the line.

Single/double spaced: the gap needed between lines of writing to allow for ascenders not to clash with descenders in the row above.

"x" height: the area where the main body of the letter stays, not counting the ascenders or descenders; the single space between the most important lines.

Getting started: Pen patterns

*G*et to know your pen. It has a broad, chisel-shaped edge, so, unlike the more familiar ballpoint, you need to ensure that the whole edge stays in contact with the paper during writing. Try these pen exercises and gain some border patterns at the same time. The patterns take you through different pen angles, which affect the shapes made. An ability to control your pen angle prepares you for Italic lower case and Gothic at 45°, Foundational, Roman and Italic capitals at 30°, and Uncial at 15°.

All these patterns will work best with lines four times the width of your pen, that is, four "nib-widths". "Nib-widths" are how we gain the right thickness for the letters, and are shown in this book for every alphabet.

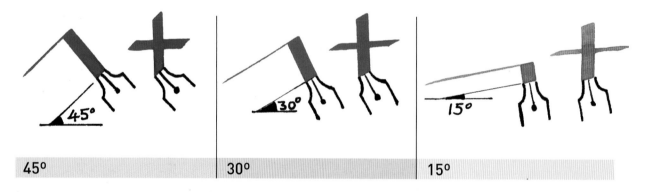

45° | **30°** | **15°**

1. For 45°, both upright and horizontal strokes should come out the same thickness; then try zigzags using the thinnest and thickest strokes.

2. For 30°, the nib is flatter to the writing line and upright strokes will come thicker than horizontal strokes (check you aren't changing the angle as you change direction).

3. Now even flatter, for 15°; the horizontal lines are even thinner and the uprights are thicker.

Opposite page
Top: 45° pen angle patterns
Middle: 30° pen angle patterns
Bottom: 15° pen angle patterns

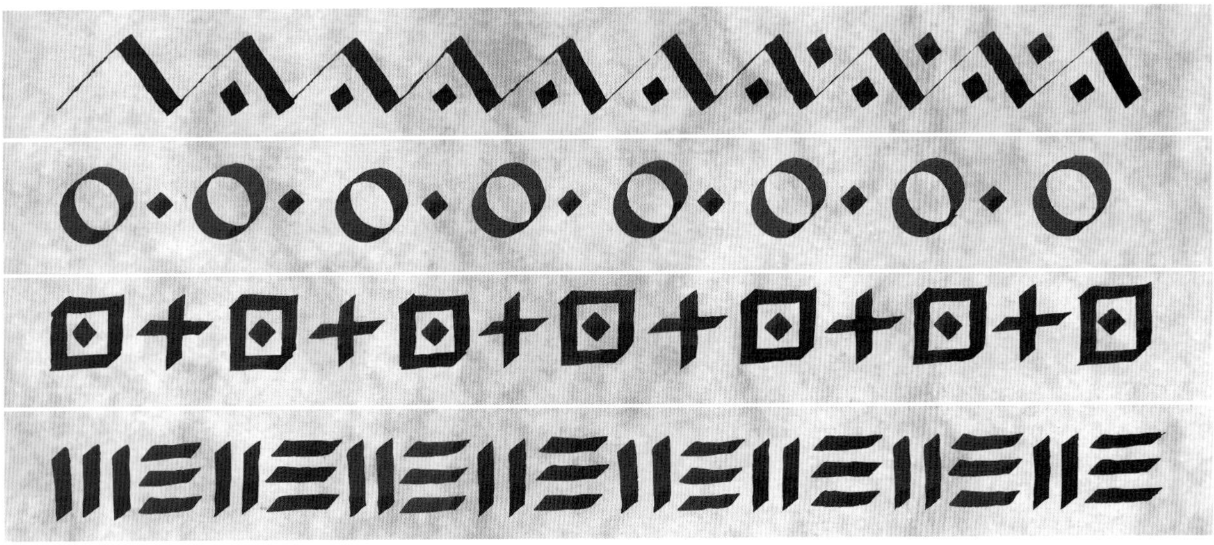

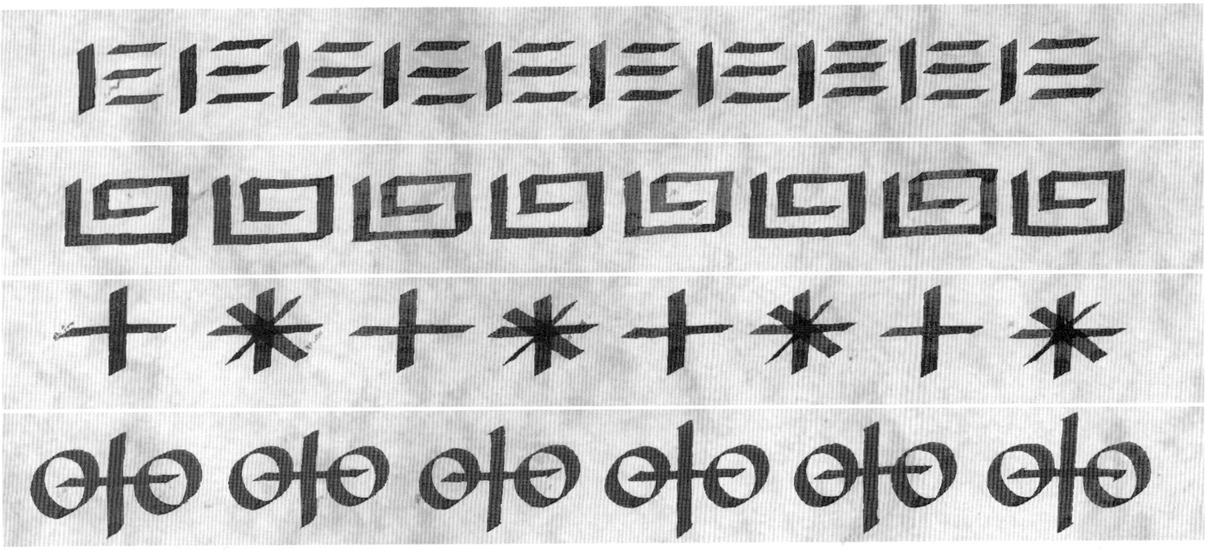

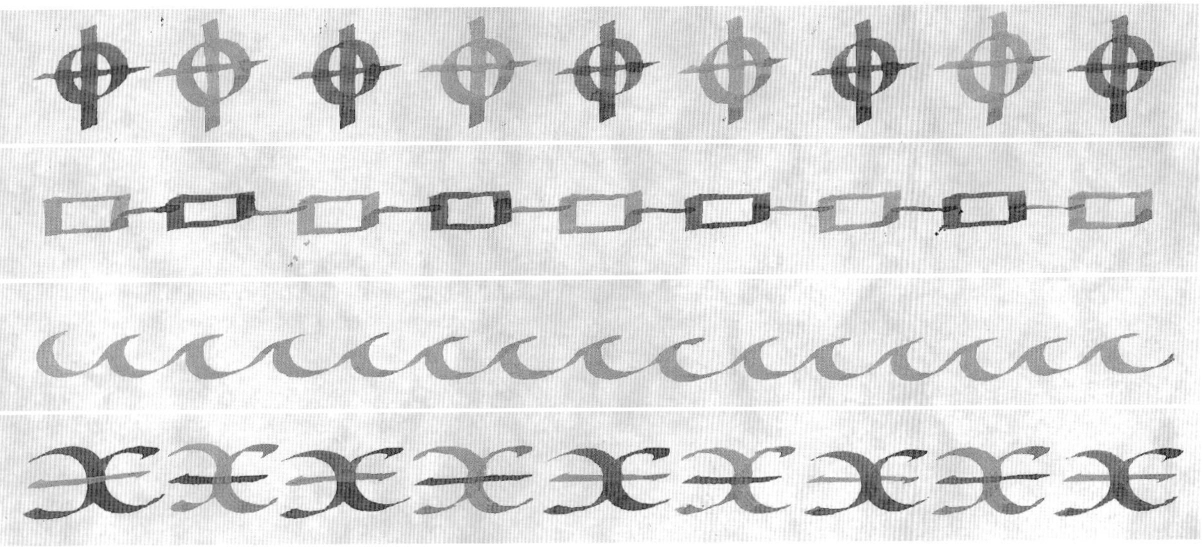

How to study different letterforms

There are many styles of writing provided in this book. They will be appropriate for different occasions, but do not be tempted to switch from one to another rapidly, as you will find they all become homogenized with little understanding of the core characteristics that make each of them different. Consider each alphabet style as a completely separate language; mix them indiscriminately and you will get a curious mixture that does not do justice to any of them.

Family characteristics

In order for a letterform to work as a unified whole, each of the 26 letters needs to have some passing resemblance to its fellows. The commonest unifying feature is a constant pen angle and x-height (all fitting within the same lines, written with the same pen, at the same angle). Look what happens when the same letter is written at different pen angles.

Note what happens when the same letters are written at the same height but with different pen nib sizes.

But there is more; in lower case letterforms, the governing letter is often O, such as in Foundational, Uncial and Gothic. All the O's have very different forms, and are repeated in the other letters, by way of their width, roundness or compactness, smoothness or angularity, and so on.

In Italic forms, the governing letter is "a", because the branching arches and the way everything has an up-and-down rhythm, is what makes it different from all the others.

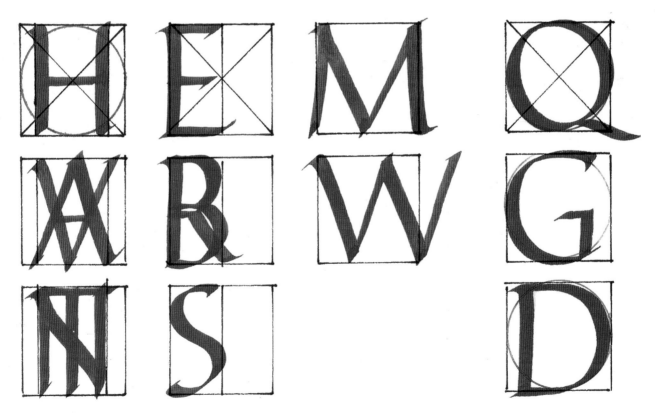

Most capital forms are derived from the original Roman Capitals, and those Romans favoured a geometrical approach, thus the letters are defined in proportions, based on the square and circle and parts thereof.

When you have studied a hand in detail, you will soon begin writing words, then sentences, and at this point you need to train your eye to notice the gaps between letters, words and lines of writing.

rain

rain

LATIN

LATIN

Letter spacing

Lower case letters have a rhythm of regular vertical strokes. Once you are aware of this, you will soon spot holes in your spacing; check by looking at it upside down, as you will stop reading the words and be assessing areas of black and white. Some letters come with their own spacing devices—"r" has it to the right, "t" has it both sides, "l" has none. Thus, you need to give space where none is integral, and watch out that those with spacers do not take more than they need.

onc advis a trop
son fait la prem
arretier devant gu
onc advis a trop
son fait la prem
arretier devant gu

Word spacing

The gaps between words need to be a little more than that provided for between the letters, but not so much that, in a page of writing, they leave "rivers" of white down the page. A general rule might be, the width of the O in your alphabet for the space between words.

Est modus in rebus, sunt certi denique fines,
Quos ultra citraque nequit consistere rectum.
Misce stultitiam consiliis brevem: dulce est

Line spacing

If writing a whole page or block of text, in lower case, sufficient space must be left between lines to allow the reader's eye to travel without confusion across the page. If there are more than 8 words to a line, check that the interline space is greater than the "x" height. The script's length of ascenders and descenders will be a determining factor, as they must have room to avoid clashing.

Est modus in rebus,
sunt certi denique fines
Quos ultra citraque

Shorter lines of text can afford to be more closely spaced.

EST MODUS IN REBUS,
SUNT CERTI DENIQUE FINES
QUOS ULTRA CITRAQUE

Capitals, which have no ascenders or descenders, can be put much closer together.

Margins

The final consideration, when you have a quantity of writing, is how to place it on the page for best effect. Always leave plenty of white space around all the writing. When you are ready to think about how the writing looks on the whole page, refer to "Laying out a page" for some ideas.

Uncials

This is a useful first alphabet to try, as it is a "majuscule" (capital). It has no "minuscule" (lower case) to accompany it, because it originates from the 3rd century. It uses the flattest pen angle, 15°, and is very rounded—think "fat and flat". Rule lines 4 times the width of your nib, (4 "nib-widths") and leave the same gap between lines of writing.

Try to find the secret "O" in every letter—if only in its width—see diagram below.

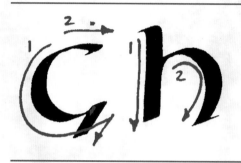

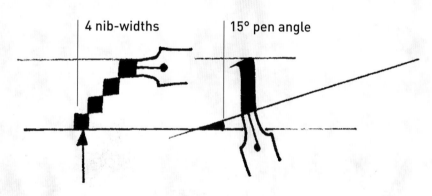

4 nib-widths   15° pen angle

all related to "O"   find C,E,G,T

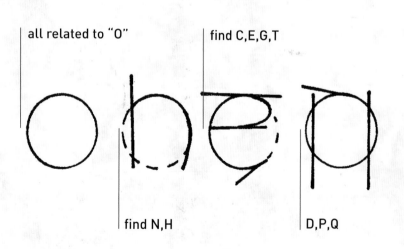

find N,H   D,P,Q

15

Foundational hand

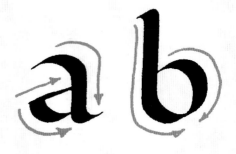

*L*ike the Uncials, these letters are very round (still look for the "o"), but with very definite ascenders and descenders, making this a "minuscule" (lower case) script. Modelled on a 10th century hand, it remains a favourite in modern font design.

The pen angle here is 30°, steeper than for Uncials, but still 4 nib-widths high. Leave a double gap between writing though, to allow for those extending ascenders. Notice particularly the way "n" and "m" are constructed, with high arches (see diagram). Use Roman capitals with this alphabet.

4 nib-widths (ascenders & descenders 3 more)

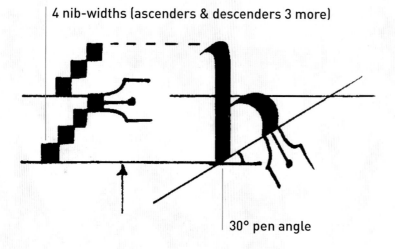

30° pen angle

related to o   how a fits o

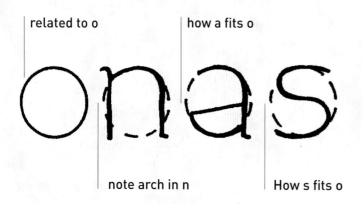

note arch in n   How s fits o

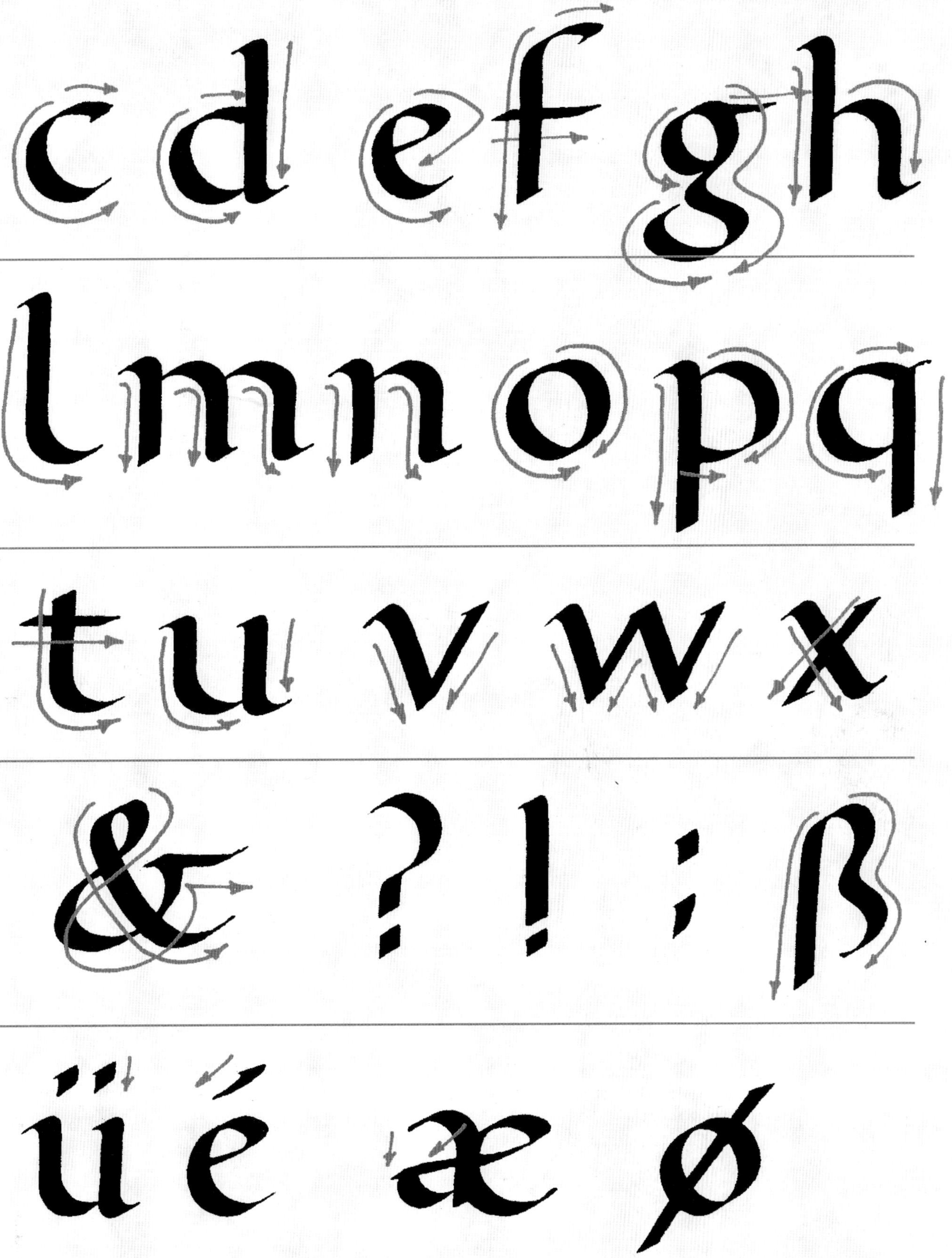

c d e f g h

l m n o p q

t u v w x

& ? ! ; ß

ü é æ ø

Roman capitals

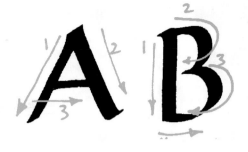

*A*s with the Foundational alphabet, keep to a 30° pen angle. These are our oldest favourite letterforms, originating 2000 years ago and still in common use. Here we use 6 nib-widths if using it with Foundational, otherwise you can use 7 or 8 for lighter looking letters. Pay close attention to the WIDTHS of these letters, as unlike the lower case, they vary to suit the sensitivities to geometry of the Roman craftsmen who perfected them. Try them out first in pencil outline in width groups (see diagrams).

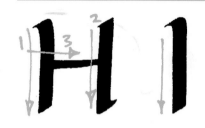

6 nib-widths   **30° pen angle**

circular:
O,Q,C,G,D

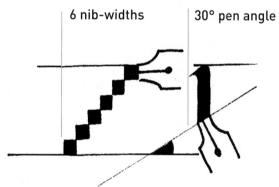
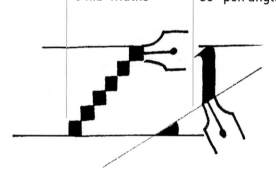

width: E,F,L,K are ½ width

M fits square, W is wider

width: H,A,V, N,T,U,X,Y,Z are ¾ width

width curved: B,P,R,S,J are ½ width

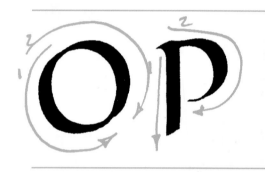

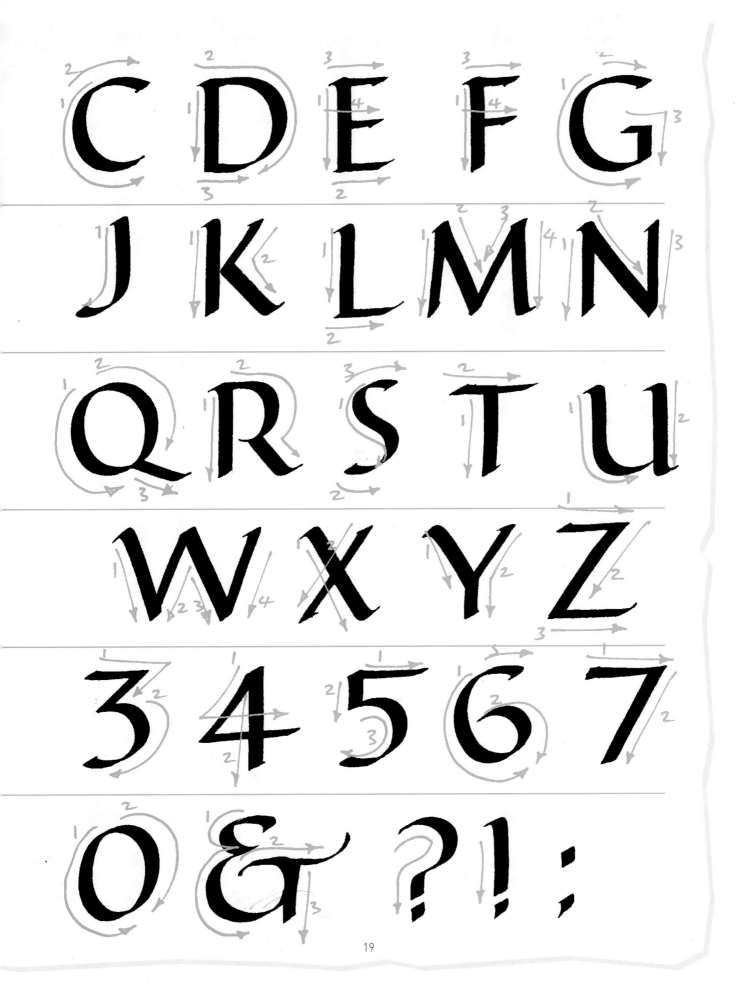

Rustics

These capitals do not have a lower case version, and are modelled on letterforms common in 5th century Italy. They are a curiosity in requiring a much steeper pen angle than for other alphabet forms, giving thin uprights and heavy tops and bottoms, a feature to be avoided in most styles. There is careful blending from the thin downstroke to the broad base serif, generally achieved by manipulating (twisting) the pen, and a general appearance of heavy diagonals. Thus the pen angle varies from very steep (60°) to fairly flat (40°). Their chief appeal is their lively, informal elegance, suitable for titles.

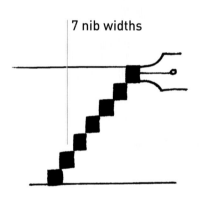

7 nib widths

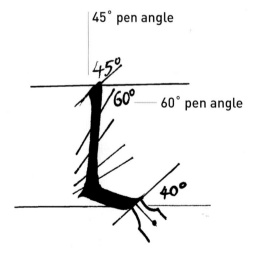

45° pen angle

60° pen angle

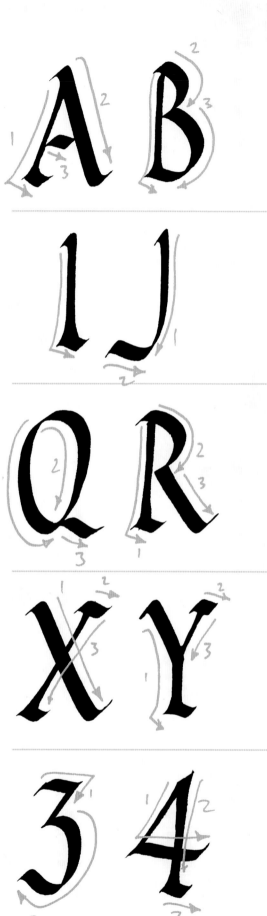

C D E F G H
K L M N O P
S T U V W
Z & ?!! 12
567890

Versals

These are essentially Roman capitals, drawn with a narrow pen. The exemplar shows double strokes where a broad pen would have created a thick stroke; in reality you would then fill this in with a third stroke to make a solid letter (and thus hide the construction). The hairline serifs complete the elegance. This basic construction then allows for variation of thickness, from very fine, with strokes close together, to heavyweight (so that several strokes would be needed for infilling, or more usefully, painted with a brush). This style was popular in medieval times; today we follow the same construction and create modern versions.

The narrow pen is held mainly vertically and horizontally, for fine lines and full thickness of the narrow pen, with some manipulation at joins.

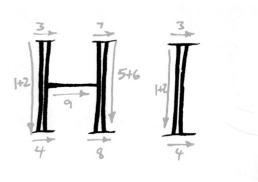

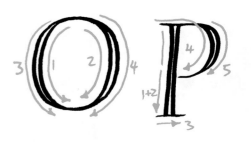

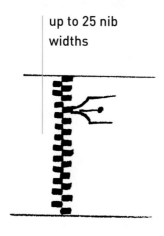

up to 25 nib widths

pen angles vary from 0° to 90°

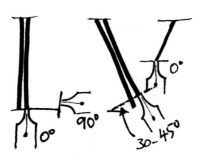

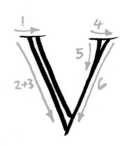

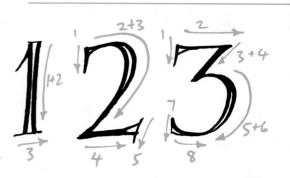

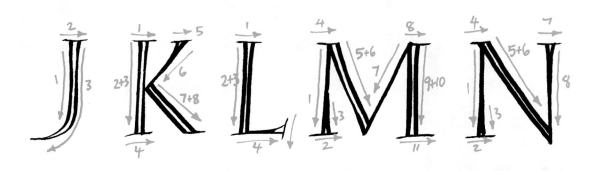

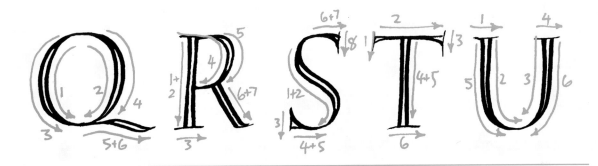

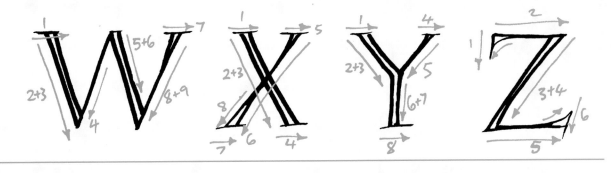

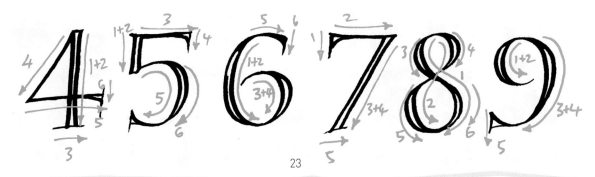

Gothic

Forty to forty-five degrees is the usual pen angle for these very angular letters, and 5 nib-widths gives some height to compensate for the narrowness. Keep the white space inside the letters the same thickness as the letter stroke. Developed in Medieval times, these letters are densely packed and should look like a row of evenly-spaced fence palings, so some letters touch.

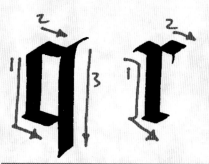

5 nib-widths

40—45° pen angle

single spaced (minimal ascenders/descenders)

note angular construction

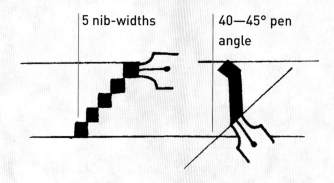

keep space inside very narrow

c d e f g h

k l m n o p

s t u v w x

& ! ? : ø æ

3 4 5 6 7 8 9

Gothic capitals

These very decorative letters must be used sparingly, never as whole words; think of them as the gates in the picket fence of lower case writing. They are wide and flamboyant, but need the same care in construction. Their roundness is best achieved with a 30° pen angle, and they should be 1 or 2 nib-widths higher than the lower case.

7 nib-widths | **30° pen angle**

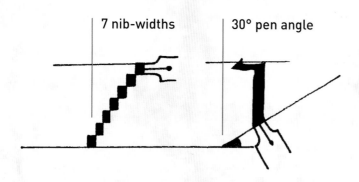

many letters based on O, C,E,G,T,Q

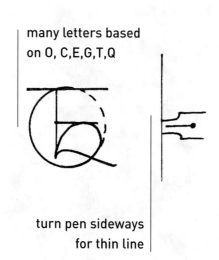

turn pen sideways for thin line

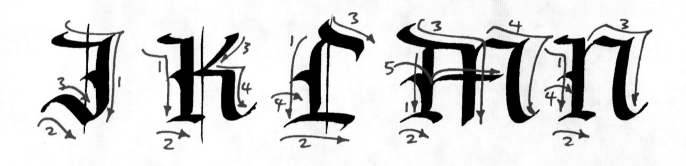

Gothic cursive

This letterform has its origins in late 15th century France, and combines the boldness of Gothic with a more flowing, up-and-down rhythm that later became characteristic of Italic. Its other name is Bastarda. The ascenders and descenders are shallow, and the body height of the letters is just 3½ nib-widths, creating a solid appearance, and the rhythmic, cursive nature encourages joining-up of some letters when writing a block of text.

The pen angle varies between 30° and 45°, requiring some manipulation (slight twisting) of the pen.

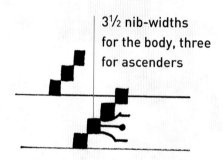

3½ nib-widths for the body, three for ascenders

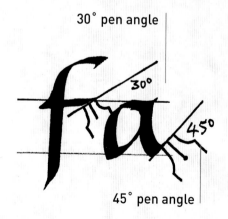

30° pen angle

30°

45°

45° pen angle

Gothic cursive capitals

These are fun letters to explore, and are more casual-looking than the Gothic capitals. Use them with the lower case letters; do not attempt to write whole words in these capitals, as they will be very difficult to read. They are heavyweight (5 nib-widths) to match the lower case letters, and have a flowing quality which is appealing for informal occasions. As in the lower case, the pen angle can vary with manipulation, but averages at 30°.

The numerals are small, to fit with the lower case, and are constructed with economy of strokes in the restricted space.

5 nib-widths

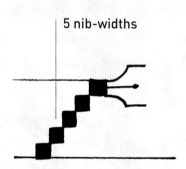

30° pen angle

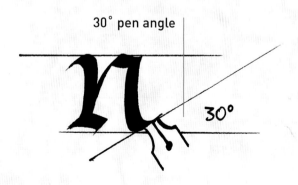

30°

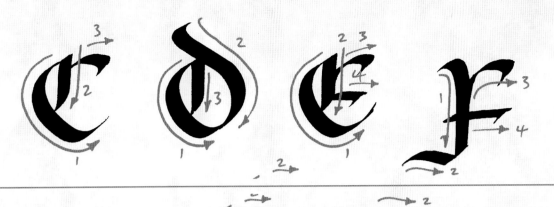

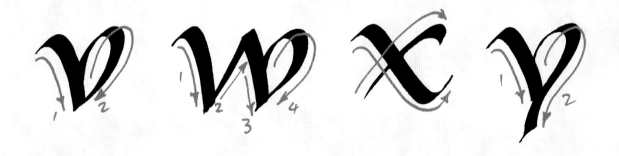

Italic

This letterform emerged in 14th–15th century Italy and remains a popular and adaptable script.

The minuscules (lower case) should all fit the "a" and "o" width, excepting "m" and "w" which are wider. They slope forward slightly. The "branching" or "springing" arches are a critical feature, made without taking the pen off (see diagram). Keep to 45° pen angle and use 5 nib-widths, with a double gap between lines for those ascenders and descenders.

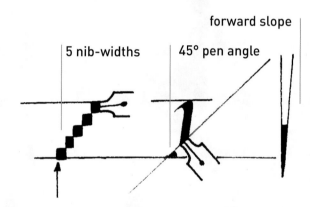

forward slope

5 nib-widths | **45° pen angle**

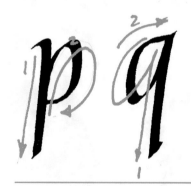

a is made taking pen to top line and down again

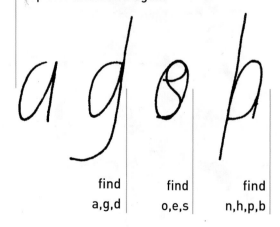

find
a,g,d

find
o,e,s

find
n,h,p,b

c d e f f g

j k l m n o

r s t u v w

z !?; ß & æ

33

Italic capitals

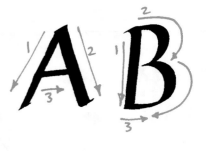

These are for use with the Italic minuscules but they are an adaptation of Roman Capitals so they are written at 30°, not 45° as might be supposed. Use 7 nib-widths (2 more than the lower case). They are compressed, slanted capitals, so their relative widths are less obvious.

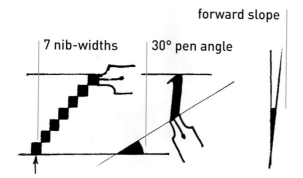

7 nib-widths   30° pen angle   forward slope

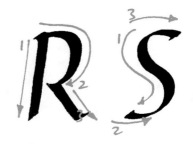

relate letters to sloping O

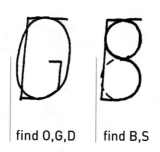

find O,G,D   find B,S

C D E F G H

L M N O P Q

T U V W X Y

1 2 3 4 5 6

9 0 & ! ? ;

Flourished italic

*F*lourishing can add elegance to a piece, as long as it is not overdone. Do not attempt to write these until the standard version is well understood. For maximum effect, the ascenders or descenders should have extra room, compared with the standard version, and any loops incorporated must be generous (larger than the bowl of the letter). The best results are obtained when flourishing is used with restraint, in combination with the standard formal version. The broad, confident strokes need a smooth-flowing pen, well charged with ink for lubrication.

The body height is 5 nib-widths, but allow at least 8 nib-widths for flourishing. There is a slight forward slope, and the pen is held at 45° (not 30° as in the capitals).

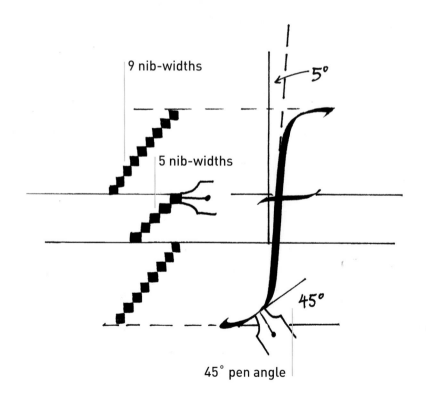

9 nib-widths

5 nib-widths

5°

45°

45° pen angle

Flourished italic capitals

*U*se these capitals with the flourished lower case, or with the formal version. They are decorative, flowing versions of the standard Italic, and are based on the Roman Capital but with extensions. It is possible to write whole words in these capitals, but you may need to lessen the extensions.

Note that the flourishes generally occur to the left of the letter, to avoid problems with spacing in a word. Maintain a steady 30° pen angle (not 45° as in the lower case) and a gentle forward slope. They are 7 nib-widths, against 5 nib-widths of the lower case.

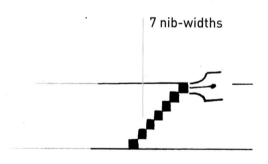

7 nib-widths

30° pen angle

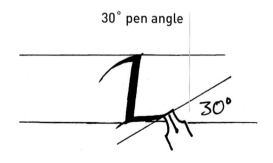

C D E F G

J K L M N

Q R S T U

X Y Z &

4 5 6 7 8 9 0

Copperplate

This script uses a quite different pen, as it requires a flexible pointed nib, similar to a "mapping pen". Unlike broad-edged pen alphabets, the thick strokes are obtained by pressing harder on the nib so that it flexes open and discharges more ink. The rhythm of writing Copperplate is "thick down, thin up" that is, applying pressure for the downstroke, easing off at the bottom, and gliding upward for a hairline upward stroke. Understandably, these nibs eventually suffer metal fatigue, so it is worth buying several at the outset.

Hold the pen so that it is parallel with the upright stroke (easier for a left-handed writer); and note that this upright stroke is actually a very steep 55° from vertical, so you may wish to turn your paper so that the slope comes more naturally.

55° writing slope

55°

c d e f g h i

l m n o p q

t u v w x y z

œ ;: !? k r 1

4 5 6 7 8 9 0

Copperplate capitals

These are very ornamental letters, and so should be used singly, to complement the lower case, not as whole words which would be unreadable. There is a basic stroke known as the "universal line of beauty" which underlies many of these letters, and is well worth studying first, in order to gain the subtlety of the change from thick to thin stroke in gentle curves. The construction of some letters is counter-intuitive, so check the arrows.

As with the lower case, there is a strong forward slope of 55° from vertical, and you might prefer to turn your paper so that you can hold the pen more comfortably.

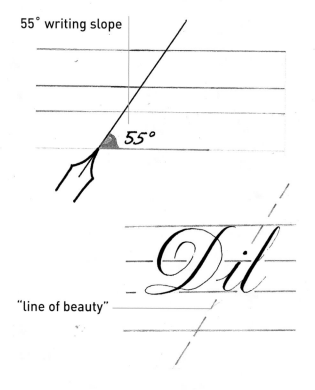

55° writing slope

55°

"line of beauty"

43

Laying out a page

For a first layout, rule up a whole page of lines, then mark out generous margins all round. As a "rule of thumb", take the gaps between writing lines as your gauge, and double this for your top and side margins; add half as much again for the bottom margin.

For better pre-planning, write all your text then cut out the lines of text in strips. Lay them on a fresh page and move them about to design your layout. Glue it when satisfied and use this as your guide for making the final "best" version.

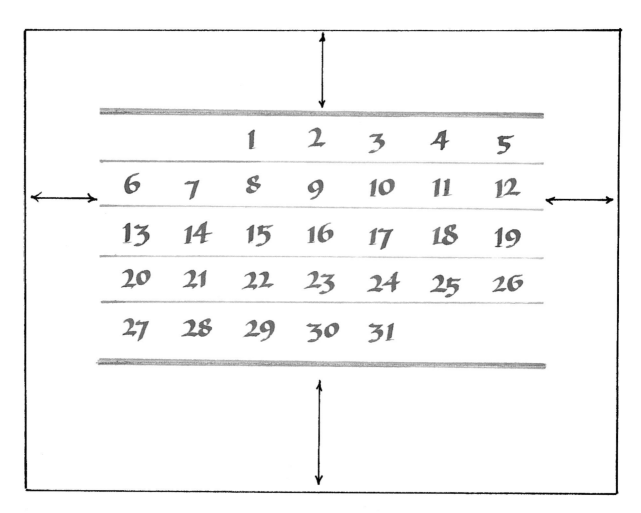

Always allow generous margins. Top and sides can have equal margins. More margin at bottom.

A lorem ipsum dolor
sit amet, consectetuer
ad sed diam non euis tin
cit ut wisi enim ad minim

Left aligned
allows for
decorative
elements.

Centered: harder to
achieve precisely so
try slight offsetting
left and right as here.
A focus point adds
visual interest.

Getting the colors you want

Whether you use colored fiber-tipped pens, inks, or paints, it helps to have a basic understanding of how colors work together, in order to create harmonious designs. Mixing colors reveals much more about their properties.

Nature gets it right; look at the leaves in Fall, how greens change to reds, which are opposite and should clash, but with many intermediate colors of orange and purple to soften the shock.

The Color Wheel

Red, blue and yellow are the "primary" colors—you can use those to make all the other colors. The color mixing wheel shown indicates how to gain the brightest "secondaries" (green, violet, orange), by using two different reds, blues and yellows, each with their bias toward that secondary. Bright secondary colors are made by mixing the two primary colors with the closest bias toward that secondary color.

Neutrals

For more subtle effects, you need to experiment
with all three primaries at once.

First, try making
gray, by mixing red,
blue and yellow; you
will need to keep
adjusting quantities.
Too green, add red;
too brown, add blue.

When you have a good
gray, add water
progressively to see its
paler versions; this is
how watercolor washes
are created.

Now try a more controlled mixing procedure, to investigate the other colors hiding in those
primaries. Mix a primary with its opposite secondary, in graduated phases from one to the other;
you will be surprised how many intermediate colors you can make, all subtle and beautiful.
Try using them in your pen, in soft combinations.

Special effects

There are many art materials and techniques that can be utilized for creating calligraphy, and here are a few of them that are particularly useful.

Art Masking Fluid

This is a rubber solution, which comes in small bottles. Decant a little into a dish and add a drop of water to make it writing consistency. Dip the pen (do not use a brush, it will be difficult to wash off) in the fluid and write with it, watching out for stringiness as the fluid dries on the pen. Leave it to dry transparent. Mix watery paint and make a wash over the area. When this is dry, rub off the masking fluid with your finger.

For extra drama, write with masking fluid on dark colored paper and paint over with white. Even very fine lines show up well.

Watercolor

Watercolors are ideal as washes for backgrounds. Use a stiff watercolor paper (300 gsm so that it will not wrinkle) and a large absorbent soft brush with plenty of water. Try any of the subtle mixtures described in the previous page, or if you have a watercolor paintbox with "earth" colors, try the following mixtures:

1. Burnt sienna, adding water to lighten.
2. Burnt sienna and cobalt (or ultramarine).
3. Raw umber and burnt sienna.
4. Burnt sienna and green.

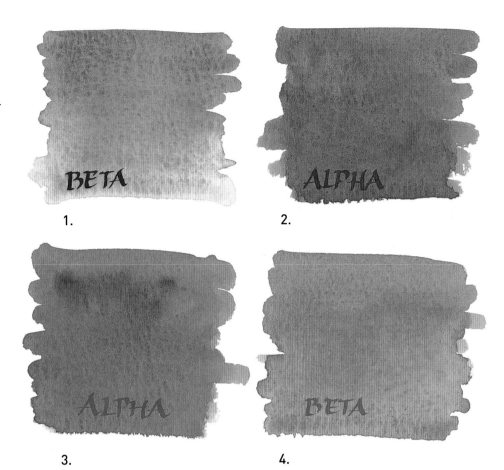

1.

2.

3.

4.

Pastels

Chalk pastels come in a wide range of colors and are ideal for thinner paper as they are a dry medium and will not cause wrinkling. Best of all, you can add them after your writing. The colors can be blended on the page by rubbing with a tissue; rub hard to press more color into the page. If you want to avoid streaks, scrape the pastel with a craft knife and rub in the resulting powder with cotton wool.

Wavy lines

This is a popular format for calligraphy, which needs some care in preparation. Start by making a pencil curve, not too pronounced, onto thin card or a cereal carton. With scissors or a craft knife, cut the curve smoothly. Use this as a template and draw the curve onto your paper. Move the template below this line, to the letter height you need, and trace again. This method can be repeated for more lines of writing, but do not make it over-complex.

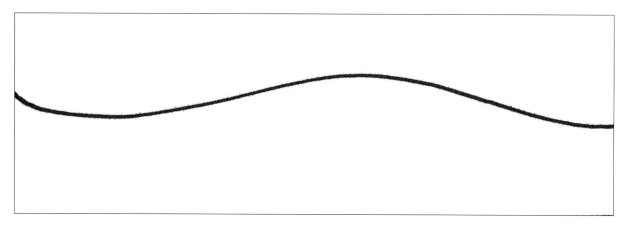

Cut a curve smoothly from thin card, with scissors or a sharp craft knife to use as your template; keep the curves shallow. Put one half aside to keep clean for ruling light lines in pencil.

LOREM IPSUM DOLOR SIT AET CONSECTETUER

Keep the wavy lines gentle, and close together. As you write, twist the paper so that the writing line allows you to keep the letters constantly upright relative to the line.

Try writing lines with a smaller gap between; this works best with scripts that have minimal ascenders and descenders. Long lines with small gaps are harder to read, so a change of weight aids reading and provides emphasis. Keep the heights the same, and use thinner and thicker nibs.

A lightweight line of text sandwiched between two shorter, heavier ones creates visual interest and would work well if the central text were a separate message from the heavy one.

With shorter amounts of writing, added interest can be made by coloring in the counter spaces of the stronger words; this increases the contrast and visually stabilizes the design to hold the lightweight floating text.

Writing in a circle

$\mathcal{U}$se a compass to mark one circle lightly. Measure the height needed for your lettering, and open out the compass to add an outer line. Do not allow the compass point to make a big hole in the center. With a ruler, mark radiating lines from the center to help with keeping the letters oriented out from the writing line.

Several trials may be necessary before you can determine the size of circle needed to fit all the words; there is no magic formula!

Make radiating lines to keep writing perpendicular to the baseline all round. Consider a central motif to cover any compass mark!

Writing in a spiral

Plan for your words to start from the center, and spiral out in a clockwise direction. Rule a line, and mark two points on it, A and B, about ½ inch apart. Place a compass point on A and open it to reach B. Mark a semi-circle (stop at the line) in a clockwise direction. Now, move the compass point to B, and open up the compass so the pencil reaches its semi-circle already made. Make the next semi-circle. Repeat this process, moving the compass point each time, until the spiral is complete. Start again at the center for adding a top line for the writing.

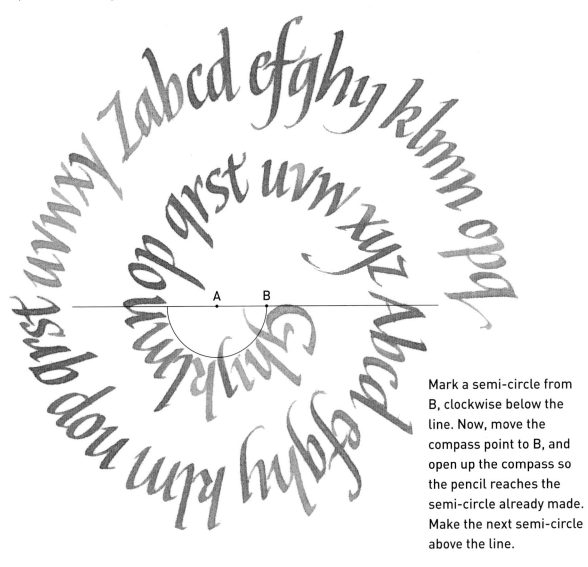

Mark a semi-circle from B, clockwise below the line. Now, move the compass point to B, and open up the compass so the pencil reaches the semi-circle already made. Make the next semi-circle above the line.

Bookmarks

*M*ake some simple gifts by experimenting with pen patterns, colors and simple calligraphy. To prolong their life and function, when completed consider taking your finished bookmarks to a copy shop to be laminated.

1. Start with the narrow lines, using a fiber-tipped pointed pen. Using one size of broad-edged pen for all the patterns, write "o" shapes with diamonds between, then add the center diamonds. Make the zigzags next, then finally the outer diamonds.

2. For a more personalized gift, try incorporating a name. Write the name first, between ruled lines. Roman capitals lend themselves to this as they have no ascenders or descenders. Start making the pattern from the end of the name. Turn it upside down and repeat the pattern from the name again.

3. If the name is short, consider repeating it. Capitals again lend themselves to incorporating borders above and below, so this is a development from (2). Prepare the name, turn over and write it again. Make the center patterns working outward from the names again. Add another row of similar pattern above and below. Coloring in with pencils can add extra interest.

4. Letterforms with ascenders or descenders provide an opportunity to use them as part of the decorative effect. Rule one set of lines for the body height only, write the name, turn it upside down and write it again on the same lines. Prepare the patterns as before, exploring variations in the colors.

1.

2.

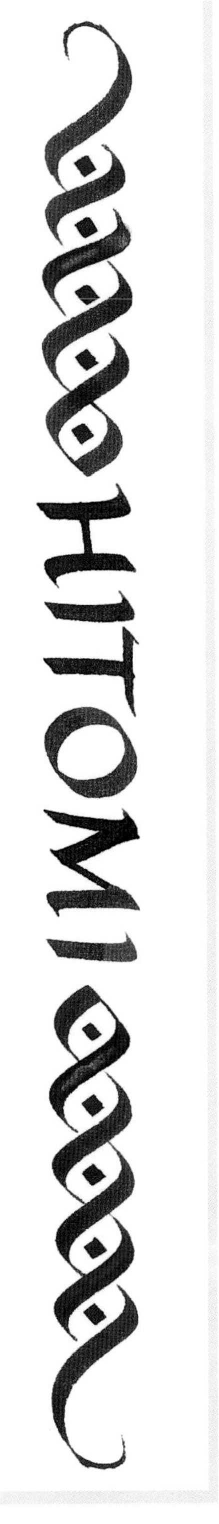

3.

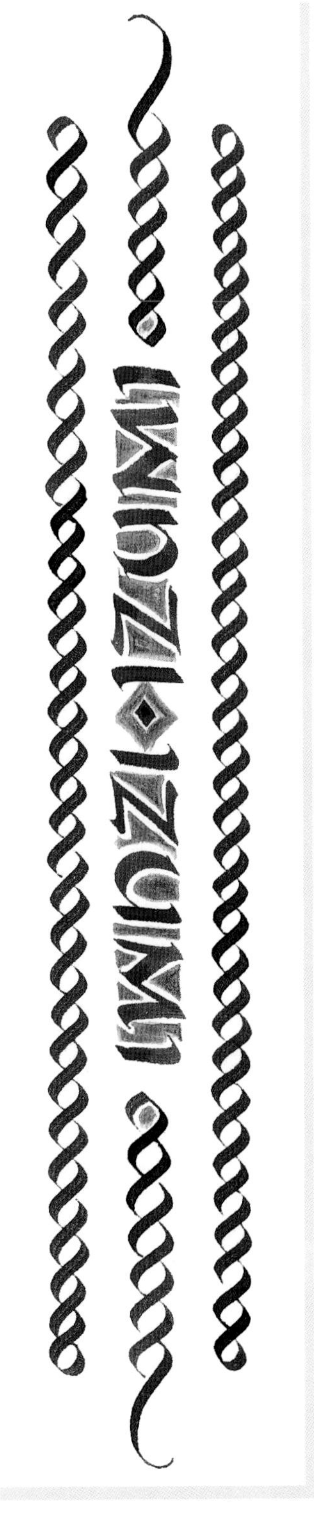

4.

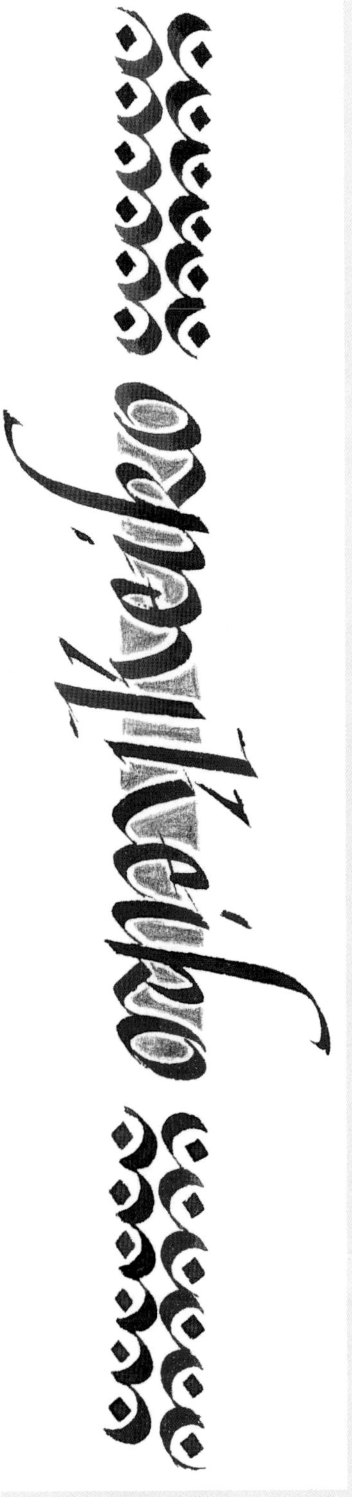

Decorative labels

abel a parcel, label a jar, your own home-made wine, your cupboards.
Organize the family's drawers, or your office shelves. Fiber tipped pens on
ready-made labels are the quickest, and then you may want to take more time for
special items of which you are proud—preserves you have prepared, a special file for
family photographs.

Room labels: make some for children, as they love to have their territory identified; choose Foundational Hand for ease of reading, and keep the design simple. Write the name in a wide pen, and add simple ruled lines or pen patterns for decoration.

Questa stanza
appartien a
ROBERTO

This room belongs to... serves as the decoration here, still with ruled lines as the plainest of edging. Make sure the name is the largest part in the design.

Jar labels: if you have made a batch of preserves, you may want to take more trouble in labelling them. Make your design with pen and ink, then take it to a copy shop and have several reduced and photocopied so that they will not smudge, and your efforts for one will serve for several jars.

If you make your own wine, all the more reason to make a special label. This design incorporates a simple drawing. If you are inexperienced in drawing, try tracing round photographs in food magazines to help you gain a simple line image which you can translate to a pen drawing. It fits better with writing if it is drawn with the same kind of movements and tool. The title is in Gothic, for density, and the "wine" outer title repeated in lightweight flourished Italic.

Decorating a letter

All the following examples take the Gothic letterform as their basis, and use art techniques to dress them up into special forms worthy of individual attention.

Write the Gothic S with a very large pen, enjoying the sweeping forms. Turn the pen sideways to gain the thin vertical line, or use a ruling pen against a ruler. Choose a soft color to fill in the counter spaces; using either watercolor pencils or thin watercolor paint, leaving a fine white line around the edge of the shape; allow the outer edges to fade out.

Write the M with a large pen, in a bright color. Using a thinner pen, and a harmonising color, write along the edge, to create an illusion of shadow. Use a very thin pen to make a final thinner line.

Write the letter in a bright color, and drop another color into it whilst wet. When dry, use a compass with a ruling pen attachment, and rule a circle that is small enough to allow the letter to burst out in places. Rule another finer line inside. Pencil in some diagonal lines, then paint with very watery colors, to fill in the background.

Examine the construction of a Versal B, but here exaggerate the widths of the structural strokes, so there are generous spaces inside. Add decorative diamond shapes to fill the open spaces. For additional interest, vary the color, and fill in some areas.

Write a letter with masking fluid, and add a ruled outline also in the fluid. When it is dry, mix watery paints of colors that will blend well together. Wet the area, and dot in the colors and watch them run. The advantage of letters with enclosed counters allows for different colors to puddle in isolation, unaffected by the outer areas.

Try the same effect but this time, when it is all dry, tidy up the outer edge with a ruling pen against a ruler, with stronger versions of the mixed colors. Explore other letters!

Using gold leaf

Gold leaf can add an extra dimension to calligraphic work with its sparkle and versatility. It can be obtained in sheets approx 3 inches square, attached to a backing paper, (usually sold in books of 25 sheets), known as "Transfer Gold", usually 23¾ carat. There are various glues for attaching it, the best for beginners being PVA (white glue).

PVA is thinned with a little water, to single cream consistency, and a dot of red paint added to color it, so that it will show up on white paper.

The PVA solution can be used in the pen, although it may blob; feed it with a brush onto the top of the pen. Here it is written on colored paper, and when dry the gold is applied after breathing all over the area. Brush away any excess with a soft brush. You can polish it carefully using the bowl of a teaspoon, through shiny paper.

The PVA mixture, now pink, is laid onto watercolor paper with paintbrush and left to dry. Breathe heavily over the area to make the surface sticky, and press the gold leaf over it; repeat in places that need touching up.

Use a technical ruling pen to apply a line of the PVA solution, and apply colored lines at either side. When dry, breathe and apply the gold as before. Whole borders could be treated in this way.

For a more subtle touch of gold, try adding some PVA to the writing ink or paint. When the word or letter is dry, breathe on it and press hard with the gold through the backing paper; you may have to repeat the process to increase coverage. The result is touches of gold but with the color still showing.

Paint the veined side of a leaf with the PVA, and press evenly on to colored paper, through tissue. Peel off carefully and leave to dry. Attach the gold in the usual way.

A square of the PVA has been painted on and left to dry. The gold has been applied as before, by breathing, working until the area is fully covered. With a blunt pointed tool, scratch lines against a ruler, making squares. Gently scratch alternate squares, to allow purchase for paint, and paint those squares with gouache.

Decorated letter with gold

A single letter decorated as an initial or as the start of a piece of work is the ideal opportunity to use a touch of gold. The term "illumination" refers to the sparkle given by the gold, so all of these will be illuminated letters. Gold paint could be substituted, but there is nothing to match the glow of the real thing!

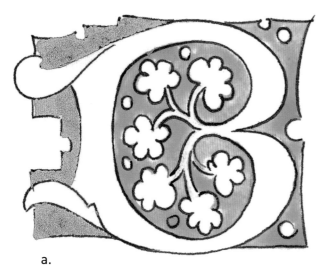

a.

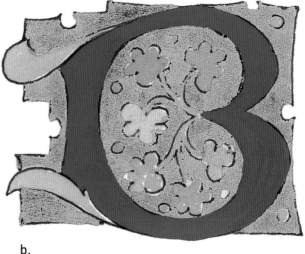

b.

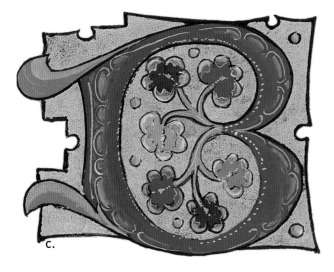

c.

A traditional illuminated letter has many stages. This one is copied from a 14th century French manuscript.

a. The outline is drawn in waterproof ink, and the glue is laid down. The gold needs to be laid before any painting, as gold may stick to paint.

b. Paint watery versions of the colors as a base, and then lay the final layer as flat color.

c. The white decorative lines are added with a fine brush with a light touch. The whole design is then strengthened with black painted outlines, again painted with a fine brush and a light touch.

A much simpler, and contemporary use of gold is to fill in the counters of a pen-written letter.

Writing with the glue takes a little more practice, but is worth the effort. Fill the pen generously with the glue, and keep refilling it but just avoiding its potential to blob. The glue may need to be thinned a little more to allow a good flow in the pen, but make sure plenty of glue is deposited in every area. When dry, breathe and lay gold as usual, and then try filling in the counters with colored pencils.

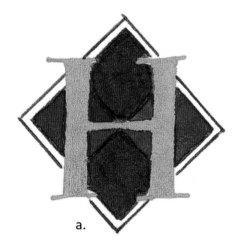

a.   b.   c.

Versal letters lend themselves particularly well to this technique of decorative initials. Three versions of H illustrate how differently the same letter can be treated, with a little imagination.

a. Trace the letter and give it extra width in the stem. With a ruler and ruling pen, add a square at right angles. Apply the gold before painting the squares.

b. Make the stems still wider, to accommodate more decoration within, and insert a gold diamond for the cross-bar. Paint the stem, and add the fine white lines with a small brush.

c. Two colors of paint, separated by a white painted line, and three gold diamonds on each stem, give a variant on the previous design.

Monograms

$\mathcal{O}$nce you have become confident with flourished capitals in Italic, a useful application for them would be to combine some for a monogram, perhaps for a letter-heading, or with an ampersand if combining two first names such as for wedding stationery. It is important to check as you make your combination, that by making joins you do not inadvertently confuse the eye into misreading the letters; aim for simplicity, and balance.

Combining H and E:

1. The first version, with no embellishments, for assessing the potential.

2. Both letters have cross-bars, so balancing them by equal extensions is a first possibility.

3. The logical development is to join the two by sharing the middle stroke, making the cross-bar continuous; this could be confusing; is it JHE?

4. Separated letters, with their flourishes to left and right for balance.

5. More emphasis on balance, counterbalancing the top left flourish in H with the bottom right flourish in E, and joined along the cross-bar.

6. No joining, and both flourishes along the bottom.

7. Introducing an ampersand (the Latin "et" meaning "and") provides extra decorative potential.

8. A final version in color.

Other examples:

VA. Two diagonal letters fit snugly together, their thin strokes adjoining and their thick strokes slightly flourished.

GA. Take care not to be tempted to combine the cross-bars of two dissimilar letters as they may create an inadvertent extra shape; instead here the cross-bars reflect each other in treatment (the flick at the left).

CSB. Here letters can provide more difficulties, particularly if they do not readily have much flourishing potential; a diagonal assembly with no attempt at embellishment is one solution.

G&F. Combining two letters that can have "descender" versions provides balance; here the ampersand is treated as a smaller item as well as being in a thinner pen.

MK. For someone's initials intended for stationery, you might consider incorporating the full name as an underlining.

Now try your own initials; first copy the flourished letters provided in the exemplar, then use thin paper (layout or tracing paper) to look at how they might be combined, before writing them out fully.

Flourishing a name

There are many occasions when you may wish to write a single word or name, and give it some extra visual interest by flourishing; on an invitation, a label, or a table place card perhaps. The ideal name would be one which has both an ascender and a descender, and maybe also a good capital that is easy to flourish.

1. Flourishing from the top of the capital, and a less conventional version of G with a flourish.

2. Another H variant, and a conventional G with more elaborate flourish, requiring a quick final stroke.

3. The plainest version, just extended descender, and extended cross-bar in the capital.

4. Ascender and descender mirrored in flourish, making a completely balanced effect.

5. Much more elaborate mirrored ascender and descender, changing the overall shape to a tall design; for most occasions, this is too overdone, and is in danger of obscuring the reading of the word in favor of its decoration.

6. Plainer variant on flourishing ascender and descender, but differing from the mirroring effect shown in no 4.

1.

2.

3.

4.

5.

6.

Anna Gerard

Viktor Wilhelm

Other examples demonstrate alternative solutions when no such evenly-balanced combination of ascender and descender occur:

ANNA. Here, no extensions whatever, so the interest lies in the capital letter; it is always advisable to make the flourishing occur to the left of the letter, to avoid interfering with the rest of the name.

GERARD. Just a flourished "d"; its position at the opposing end to the capital helps to balance the design.

VIKTOR. Here a lower-case K is serving as both ascender and descender, but beware of allowing the tail to spoil the spacing of the following letter; r at the end is allowed to extend.

WILHELM. Two ascenders adjacent can provide a problem; either keep the first one plain and flourish the second, or write them at increasing heights as shown, so they can be overlapped.

Calligram

A calligram is a picture, made from calligraphy. It can be fun to try out various shapes, and play with suitable colors. The aim is to make the whole shape in letters, although outlines or some small features drawn with the pen may help to define the subject and aid recognition.

Using different sizes of pen can aid the feeling of perspective or contour in a curved shape. First find your shape; it needs to be distinctive, and recognisable from its profile, then decide the words you will incorporate—usually a small selection of words related to the picture, that can be repeated frequently to fill the spaces.

An oak leaf has a distinctive shape that will aid the viewer's understanding. Mix a series of rich colors or select red and green inks and decant some into mixing dishes, for cross-contamination. Use two or three pen sizes for visual interest, and write some words large, others very small to fill in areas. Leaves in the Fall have inspiring colors, so be guided by them for color mix inspirations. Make sure all the inside area is filled.

A carrot with its leaves gives the opportunity for two colors and a relatively simple shape as a first attempt. Pencil the shape outline first, and write the repeated words in curves to suggest the rounded contours of the carrot. For the leaves, use the pen to make the stalks, and write "leaves" (in any language) in a small pen giving the effect of feathery ends.

A sitting cat also has a distinctive shape, but is more difficult to fill, as there are many contours to suggest with the curve of the body. Try writing the main body in a larger pen, and explore the fun of giving it a stripy tail and forelegs. The face needs its eyes and nose to be defined, do this with a middle-sized pen, and fit the contoured writing around these. To try other animal poses, find pictures in magazines or books and trace the outlines as the starting point.

Laying out pages for a book

There are simple geometry rules for ruling up pages for writing in a book, which work best where the proportions are not extreme; in the opened double page, if one side is not more than twice the other. If the latter is the case, then some adjustments need to be made for visual balance.

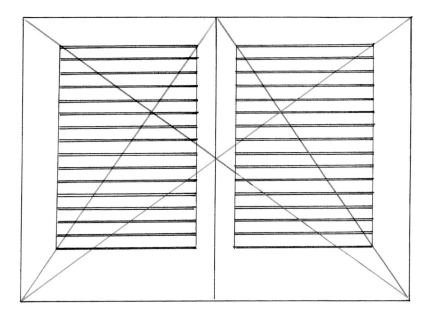

Rule lines diagonally across the whole double page, and then repeat this on the single pages. Establish the narrowest measurement in the gutter (center), and rule this. Where the gutter line meets the diagonal at the top, this marks the limit of the top margin. Rule the top margin. Where this meets the outer diagonal, mark the outer margin. Rule that. Where that line meets the diagonal, this identifies the bottom margin.

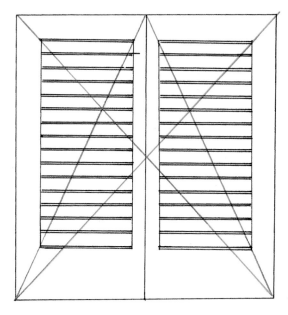

The geometry works for a layout that is rather narrower also. Of course, when you come to write your text, you may find you need to adjust the margins slightly, but the geometry may help in the outset.

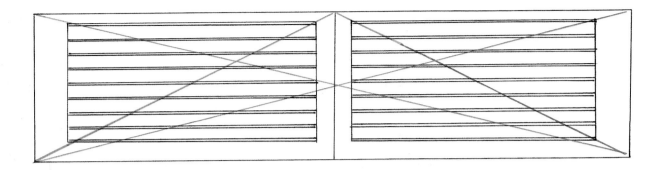

The method does not work with a very wide proportion! Here, the result is top and bottom margins are much too small.

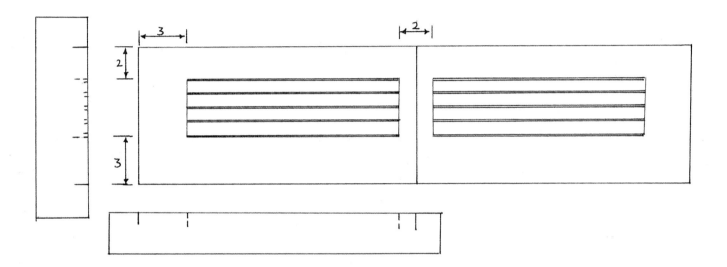

Instead, start with your desired gutter measurement, (both sides of the fold) and try using the same measurement for the top margin, then increase the side and bottom margins by about half as much again.

Once margins are established, prepare a template to ensure that every page of the book is ruled up the same way, and to save time in measuring. Prepare two cards, longer than the pages of the book, and mark all lines from top edge, through all writing lines, to bottom edge on one card, and another card for the left-to-right markings. Mark these off along the edges of all the pages and rule the lines.

Writing a small book

*B*ooks make attractive and thoughtful gifts, if the subject-matter is chosen to be important to the receiver and the first ones you try need not contain a great deal of writing. Consider, for your first book, a single line of a verse per page. The example below is an extract from a 6th century hymn in Latin.

Once confidence is gained, several pages with more text can be considered. You will need to refer to the geometry method described previously to lay out your pages.

Hunc caelum terra, hunc mare,
hunc omne quod in eis est,
auctorem adventus tui,
laudat exsultans cantico.

First, write out the full text, to establish line lengths. Consider the most suitable script, or select the one for which you have most skill. In this case, Gothic is chosen for its sympathy with Latin, and for its compact width.

Hunc caelum terra, hunc mare

For one line on a page, take the longest line of text as the gauge, and draw a rectangle around it that will accommodate the length and make attractive proportions in a book. Working backward from what is an economical shape to cut from a given paper size is another route, but do not compromise on good margins.

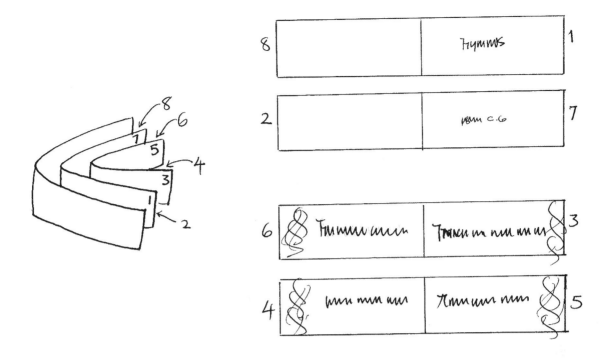

For a book that will have many pages and a cover, a rough sketch mock-up would be a wise plan, to establish how the pages fit together, should you need several sheets folded into each other. Label and number them clearly and use them as your guide when starting to write.

Rule up with a template, and write the pages. Take care to leave one side to dry before starting on the other side. Keep your rough in front of you, to avoid mistakes, as major errors could involve redoing the other side as well.

As a single line on a page can look rather lonely, consider a pattern to fill the outer margin. Link it in color to the cover choice, and in style to the lettering used. Here a vine pattern has been used on a rubber stamp, and the stamp printed three times for a shadow effect; this will allow for variation in writing widths on the pages.

Cut colored card wider than the book pages, and sew together in the center with matching thread.

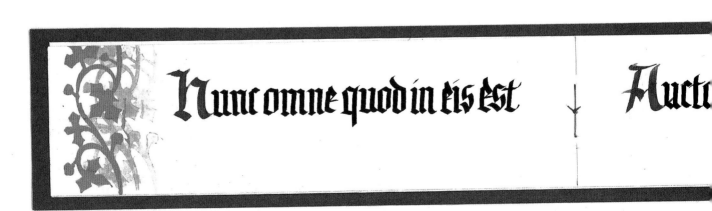

Using colored paper

Colored papers can save the trouble of creating a wash background, and come in both bright and subtle colors. Check that they accept ink or paint well before buying too much; some papers are absorbent so the writing "bleeds" and others too shiny and slippery for writing.

Investigate Ingres paper, and colored paper intended for use with chalk pastels, which has a textured and smooth side (use the latter). The following experiments use a mid-tone paper, which allows both light and dark colors to show up.

Mix a color that is darker than the paper, and is harmonious with it; or write in black. If the paper is mid-tone or lighter, you will still be able to see pencilled guide lines.

Try the same tone of paper with light and white paint. This takes time to mix the paint to a consistency that will be opaque on the paper whilst still runny enough to go through the pen. For white, "Bleedproof", white is recommended, as it is very dense.

Combining white and black on mid-tone paper can be very effective. Decide which is to take precedence. Here the black plays a supporting role to the central larger white letters.

A more complex design can be built up, again deciding which is to take precedence. The black is heavier weight than the Copperplate border, lending a decorative effect.

Mixing colors that blend well with a colored paper may take several trials. If combining two colors, the most successful combination is likely to be a light and a dark color if the paper is mid-tone, following the lesson learned with black and white. Here the yellow name is in danger of being overwhelmed by the dark pattern, but this is lightened by the addition of the additional fine line in yellow.

Color change in the pen

Writing in one color on white is often sufficient for requirements. However, for more expressive works, try writing in a series of blended colors. There are several ways of achieving this, but most important is to select colors that will mix attractively together and not turn muddy (unless browns are your goal).

EST MODUS
IN REBUS
SUNT DENIQUE
FINES CERTI
QUOS VITRA
CITRAQUE
NEQUIT
CONSISTERE
RECTUM

Alternating lines of color can provide visual interest, gentle stripes down the page. Make sure the colors go well together. These lines were mixes of Magenta and Warm Yellow.

Est modus
in rebus, sunt
denique fines

Mix two colors that together will make another, attractive color. Mix the colors in separate slots in your palette, and feed the pen with the colors consecutively, or dip indiscriminately from one to the other. The colors will blend in the pen.

Three colors take a little more trial and error. Here Magenta, warm yellow and a touch of green turns them all darker and into more neutral mixes. Again, indiscriminately dip from one color to another, ensuring an overall balance.

EST MODVS IN
REBVS, SVNT
DENIQVE FINES

Dropping-in colors is less predictable, and best used for large letters where you can see what you are doing. One letter needs to be done at a time, ensuring that it is kept wet for long enough to drop in the second color so that it runs. Check that the colors will mix harmoniously. It may help to write in the lighter color and drop in the darker, to avoid swamping one with the other.

Overlaying colors

Explore the possibilities of writing in very pale, watery colors, as an all-over background texture, or a faint pattern. When it is dry, then stronger writing can be laid on top.

For an unusual "congratulations" card, play with positioning of a repeated message spread across a circle. Draw some guidelines that radiate from the center, and do some practice writing first to establish the lengths of words, as positioning may be critical. When all the message is complete, and dry, consider the placing of the name in stronger color—again, do some trials first.

MYSTERIEUX

Explore writing a repeated phrase, placed in a block with some interline space. When that is dry, overlap the interline space with more writing, with a bigger pen, in another watery color. When absolutely dry, and not before, or the top writing will spread, write the final top layer in the strongest color.

Mix a series of subtle colors, here based on neutral greens, and water some of these down until very thin. Write the chosen word in Gothic several times down the page, leaving a gap; turn upside down and repeat in the gaps. Turn sideways and write over, when previous layer is dry, in Copperplate. When all is dry, spray the surface with hairspray to fix it and prevent the top layer bleeding, and write the top message in a stronger color.

Alphabet design

Once a full alphabet has been practiced and become familiar, it can be very rewarding creating a design using all the letters. Select a script that particularly appeals, and explore the possibilities.

Before going ahead, it can be useful to sketch out a layout in pencil, to check that the letters will fit in an orderly shape, without a lonely letter on the bottom. In the examples shown here, a single capital has been selected for special treatment; this might make a suitable gift if the recipient's initial were to be given this treatment.

Selecting a letter that occurs in the middle of the alphabet presents a design challenge in balancing the rest of the letters evenly around it. Some trials will be necessary first. When the final design and pen sizes are determined, write the central letter first. Here it is arranged to fit in the space of two lines of normal letter size, and is written in a separate color from the remaining alphabet. Notice the narrow inter-line space, to preserve the tightness of the design.

The letter A happens to be a visually interesting shape in many script styles, and so it lends itself to this treatment. Note as before, the close interline spacing, and the change of colors for extra interest. Take care to keep all the lines of a similar width, to maintain a balanced design.

Simple borders

*I*f you have studied the pen patterns supplied earlier in this book, you will already have a repertoire with which to begin your borders. Explore them in various pen sizes, in order to develop an eye for scale, to help you decide how big the pattern needs to be, in relation to the image or writing inside.

This border incorporates two thin lines drawn with a ruling pen against a ruler. The semicircles are added next, in a broad pen, followed by small squares added with a very small pen.

Ruling pen outline again. The zigzag pattern is added slowly, to keep the lines even, and to negotiate the corners successfully. If corners do present a problem, then stop short of them on each side and add a different motif in each corner afterward.

A very simple design, in a pen narrower than that used for the S inside. The pattern is simple but regular.

Outline ruled after writing the flourished A. A very small pen used for writing Italic capitals all round; a message or repeated name would be a suitable substitute. When dry, some chalk pastel or colored pencil rubbed over the small writing adds some extra interest.

A heavy border to enclose a heavyweight capital; style of border has been chosen to reflect the letter. When completed, in order to soften the border a little, to separate it visually from the Q, water is run over it to make controlled smudging.

Borders help single items such as room numbers stand out. For added impact, the square is oriented on its point. A simple pattern of curves overlapped is creating a rope effect. Now try your own!

Simple knotwork

$\mathcal{K}$notwork is a well-known feature of Celtic tradition and is a favorite of some for decorative borders or motifs, used with the Uncial hand, which is their contemporary.

Once you understand the structure of the pattern-making, you can develop your own knot patterns, but try these first.

Celtic knotwork makes striking borders (just take care that your writing is not overwhelmed by it). Here is a border made of four strands (but you could explore three). Rule lines equal distances apart, and mark them off in squares. Try the straight part before tackling any corners. Mark the skeleton (the shapes look like fishes) then add the flesh in pencil, before working out the over-and-under system.

For a corner, you need to break strands and turn them back on each other, and take care with the overlapping to ensure the system does not become confused.

Paint in the different strands, and fill in the counter space afterward in a harmonious color.

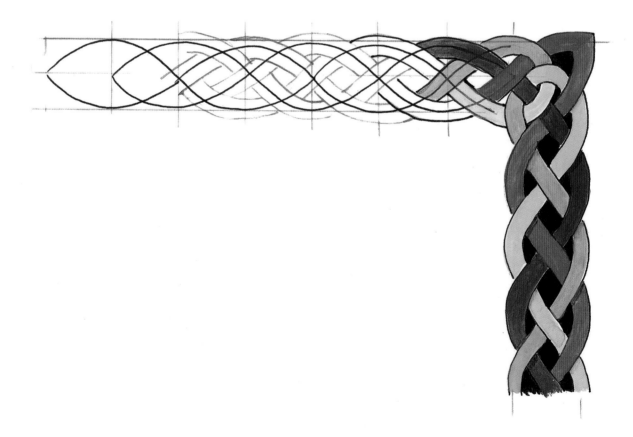

Construct a circle with a compass, and a second circle inside. Divide the circle into 4 as shown, then subdivide those right angles at 45°. Judge by eye to subdivide each section into three parts, and rule more lines. (Alternatively, use a protractor to mark out 15° intervals).

Mark a skeleton line curving from the outer mark to three lines along, on the inner mark, and continue up and down round the circle. Do the same with the next curve, noting where it begins, always going across two lines. There are three strands; the third line should be simpler to plot, as it copies the others.

Now "flesh out" the skeletons in pencil, to give thickness. If you use pencil, you can go over again in ink when you have worked out the over-and-under sequence.

When you are sure all the over-and-under sequences are right, paint each strand a different color.

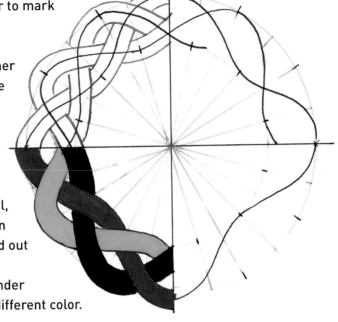

Here is how to combine such a circle with calligraphy. Some planning will be necessary to fit the words you want to use around the circle. Write in colors that fit with those you plan to use in the knotwork. It is advisable to rule all the lines and do the writing before the knotwork, in case of spelling errors.

Eye-catching envelopes

Make a splash with your correspondence and play a little with designs. Envelopes are an economical way to have fun with a temporary medium that can help you to practice design solutions, reacting to the names and exploring unconventional placing on the page.

Take care always to make the address clearly readable for the postal system, or your finely-crafted work of art may never reach its destination.

Powerful Gothic lettering will stand out well; remember to leave space at the top for the stamp and any franking; the address sits along the gap left by the first name being much shorter than the surname.

A short address allows it to be written in a single line across the center, with the name flourished above and below. This name has only ascenders in the top line and a descender in the bottom line, giving the opportunity for flourishing in full flow top and bottom.

Another short name, first and surname of equivalent length, here rendered in Italic capitals for a simple arrangement on a narrow envelope, balanced with the address clearly written in three lines to the right.

Taking advantage of a freely-written y at the end, this name has to be pushed to the left corner to allow for a dynamic arrangement with the address started below the name, aligned along the stroke of the y to emphasize the daring layout.

A name with similar length in first and surname, and short enough to try a counter-balanced arrangement of two blocks. The name is written in Uncial with a large pen, a second color dropped in to the first whilst it is still wet. The address is written in a lightweight version of Uncial for more contrast, and arranged in a block to reflect the shape of the name.

Quotation

The challenge with any quotation is how to display it to best advantage. It is worth trying out two different approaches to a design, in order to broaden the possibilities; try a vertical and horizontal layout, to explore the best options.

It is best to write out the full quotation on rough paper first, to assess the volume of text, and then try breaking it into groups that will provide balanced line lengths.

For this design, using Rustics, a motif based on Roman patterning has been incorporated, and a rubber stamp made, to provide the chance to repeat the pattern.

To cut the rubber stamp from this pattern, make an accurate tracing of the pattern with an HB pencil. Transfer the design to the surface of a plain plastic eraser by pressing it firmly over the design. If necessary, reinforce the lines by marking directly on the eraser with the pencil.

Use a sharp craft knife, or a fine lino-cutting tool, to cut out the shapes; take care to know which parts should stay. Use a colored stamp pad to check the result.

This design employs the rubber stamp all round as a border, using two colors of ink, lightly stamped. Do the writing first, and establish the border measurements afterward, to avoid any mismatch. Where the lines of text are significantly shorter, there is space to infill with one more stamp.

EST MODUS
IN REBUS,
SUNT CERTI
DENIQUE FINES
QVOS VITRA
CITRAQVE
NEQUIT
CONSISTERE
RECTUM

H O R A C E

This design is more complex, using two sizes of pen and a centerd arrangement that needs some tight planning. The decoration is minimal, strengthening the central alignment and assisting the balance. A larger rubber stamp adds weight at the top, to help balance the heavier writing on the lower half. The small stamp completes the design under the credit.

Writing on fabric

There are many opportunities to write on fabric, which would make gifts such as monogrammed handkerchiefs, tablecloth, or T shirts. You need a nylon broad-edged brush, not sable as this is too floppy, not bristle as this is too stiff. Poly-cotton is an ideal fabric, but you could explore others. If the fabric will be washed, then use fabric paints (but not silk paints, as these are designed to spread) or household emulsion or latex paint if just rainproofing is required.

FELIZ CUMPLEAÑOS

Feliz cumpleanos—happy birthday. A birthday tablecloth could be fun and informal. Cut some cheap cloth to size, and chalk some guidelines along the edges. Write your repeated message all round the edge of the tablecloth, and iron it to fix the color. Fray the edges or machine hem.

Gothic capitals are attractive decorative features, and worth trying out with the brush. Q is particularly satisfying, with that long diagonal sweep. Here the counter spaces have been painted in with a narrow pointed brush, for added interest.

The Italic form lends itself well to brush writing. Take care always to fill the brush and then wipe the edge to a sharp chisel profile before writing, otherwise the sharp serifs will not be successful.

Color change in the brush is possible, and gives another dimension to the letters. Charge the brush with yellow paint, wipe the edge to its chisel, touch one side in the red paint, wipe again, and write.

These letters are painted with a pointed brush. Poly-cotton is thin enough to see through and trace the letters from an exemplar; paint the letters carefully and then add some color in the counters. Try mixing yellow one end of the counter and orange on the other.

Wrapping paper

Kraft paper is very sturdy material for wrapping parcels, but lacks the party spirit. Personalize your parcel by creating your own decoration, using just lettering. The examples shown here use green kraft paper; you may be able to find red also, but this will work just as well with the original brown version.

The paints can be gouache if the parcel is not going to be exposed to damp, but if you need it to be smudge-proof then use household emulsion or latex paint and black waterproof ink. Just two sizes of pen are used in these three examples.

Using a large pen and plenty of white paint, feeding the pen frequently, write in heavy-weight Italic across the paper, repeating the message. Leave a gap, and repeat the line, but make sure it is staggered, so that the start of a word comes under the middle of the word above. Continue down the paper in the same way.

Write the repeated message across the paper as the previous page, with heavy weight writing, leaving even gaps between the lines. When it is dry, repeat the message with black ink in a thinner pen, filling the space in between, creating contrast by using very lightweight lettering in the other color.

Writing both ways gives a pattern to the writing, reducing the readability but adding to the decorative result. Lightweight flourishing is used here, with the flourishes exaggerated, to overlap and add to the free flowing appearance, to give a joyful impression. Write repeatedly one way, with regular gaps, then when it is dry, turn it upside down and repeat the same pattern across the first lines.

Small writing

Writing at anything shallower than 4mm high needs some practice, as it is still important to retain thick and thin strokes and maintain the letterform. Sometimes the ink or paint will need thinning to avoid a monoline, or different paper chosen that responds better to your ink. The serif (entry and exit tick) needs to be kept to a minimum, so as not to take up too much of the proportion of the stroke.

Explore the possibilities of white and black on a mid-tone paper; the white needs good opacity. This credit, whilst not as small as the version below written with a Copperplate pen, still requires a light touch and sharp writing. The quality of the paper may be a factor in achieving this.

Roman capitals can be very effective at small sizes, provided you write with a light touch, so that the serifs are minimal, and cross-bars are not too thick. Using color on colored paper requires a good consistency of paint for opacity. The credit, in white, is written with a copperplate nib with a very light touch.

Hunc caelum, terra, hunc mare hunc omne quod in eis est, auctorem adventus tui laudat exsultans cantico

Copperplate is a popular choice for small writing, because the nib is very fine and invites thin hairlines. The variable pressure needed to write this script makes the thick and thin strokes; care is necessary with the consistency of the ink or paint.

Hunc caelum, terra, hunc mare, hunc omne quod in eis est, auctorem adventus tui laudat exsultans cantico

Fitting a message in a small space, perhaps a poem or quotation inside a card, asks for small writing. Think about the overall shape and plan for any flourishes to occur in the outer regions.

Further techniques

Try a repeated word radiating from the center, for decorative effect. A name for a greetings card might be suitable. Rule lines at right angles, then add a top line for the "x" height. Start from the center and write outward; turn the paper and repeat the process three more times.

Color in the shapes in the initial letter only, to maintain the central focus.

Numerals do not receive the attention they deserve, so try making them into a feature, perhaps for a birthday or anniversary.

First write the number, then color in a square area around it, leaving a neat white gap. Now use a pointed pen, or preferably a technical ruling pen, to rule colored lines top and bottom. Finally add some festive swirls and dots to complete the design.

...and finally

Here we have covered just a few scripts and techniques to get you started. Find a class to help you develop your skills, share ideas and build your confidence, or find out what calligraphy societies operate in your area. Have fun, and keep writing!